Sea Horses

by Christina Leaf

BELLWETHER MEDIA • MINNEAPOLIS, MN

Note to Librarians, Teachers, and Parents:

Blastoff! Readers are carefully developed by literacy experts and combine standards-based content with developmentally appropriate text.

Level 1 provides the most support through repetition of high-frequency words, light text, predictable sentence patterns, and strong visual support.

Level 2 offers early readers a bit more challenge through varied simple sentences, increased text load, and less repetition of high-frequency words.

Level 3 advances early-fluent readers toward fluency through increased text and concept load, less reliance on visuals, longer sentences, and more literary language.

Level 4 builds reading stamina by providing more text per page, increased use of punctuation, greater variation in sentence patterns, and increasingly challenging vocabulary.

Level 5 encourages children to move from "learning to read" to "reading to learn" by providing even more text, varied writing styles, and less familiar topics.

Whichever book is right for your reader, Blastoff! Readers are the perfect books to build confidence and encourage a love of reading that will last a lifetime!

This edition first published in 2017 by Bellwether Media, Inc.

No part of this publication may be reproduced in whole or in part without written permission of the publisher. For information regarding permission, write to Bellwether Media, Inc., Attention: Permissions Department, 6012 Blue Circle Dr., Minnetonka, MN 55343.

Library of Congress Cataloging-in-Publication Data

Names: Leaf, Christina, author.
Title: Sea Horses / by Christina Leaf.
Description: Minneapolis, MN : Bellwether Media, Inc., [2017] | Series:
    Blastoff! Readers. Ocean Life Up Close | Audience: Ages 5-8. | Audience: K to
    grade 3. | Includes bibliographical references and index.
Identifiers: LCCN 2015048432 | ISBN 9781626174207 (hardcover : alk. paper)
ISBN 9781618912671 (paperback : alk. paper)
Subjects: LCSH: Sea horses–Juvenile literature.
Classification: LCC QL638.S9 L43 2017 | DDC 597.6798–dc23
LC record available at http://lccn.loc.gov/2015048432

Table of Contents

What Are Sea Horses?

thorny sea horse

Sea horses are unusual fish. They have horselike heads! Their eyes can move in different directions at the same time.

These fish swim upright using fins on their backs and heads.

long-snouted sea horse

Bony plates protect sea horses' long, curvy bodies. Males have soft pouches on their bellies.

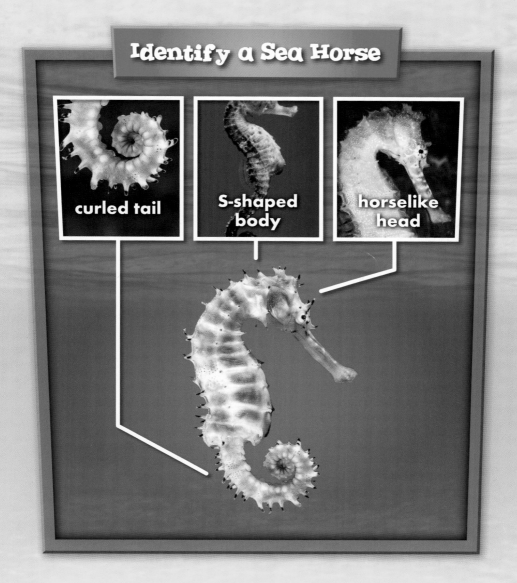

Identify a Sea Horse

curled tail

S-shaped body

horselike head

At the end of sea horse bodies are **flexible**, monkeylike tails. The tails have a boxy shape for a strong **grip**.

7

There are more than
45 types of sea horses.
Some are over 1 foot
(30 centimeters) long!

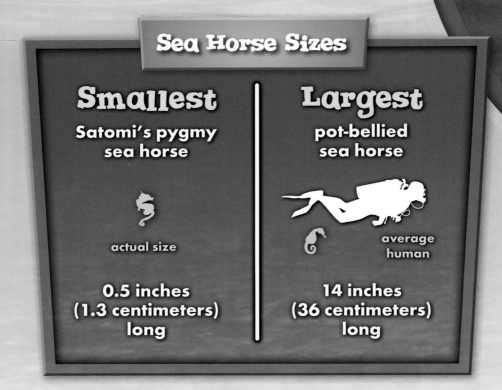

Sea Horse Sizes

Smallest

Satomi's pygmy
sea horse

actual size

0.5 inches
(1.3 centimeters)
long

Largest

pot-bellied
sea horse

average
human

14 inches
(36 centimeters)
long

pot-bellied
sea horse

Satomi's pygmy
sea horse

However, many are just a few inches long. Most sea horses weigh less than 1 pound (0.4 kilograms).

In the Shallow End

Shallow waters along coasts provide homes for sea horses. Most live around the **tropics**, but some are found in cooler waters.

spiny
sea horse

COMMON SEA HORSE

life span:
1 to 5 years

depth range:
**0 to 26 feet
(0 to 8 meters)**

common sea horse range =

conservation status: **vulnerable**

Extinct	Extinct in the Wild	Critically Endangered	Endangered	Vulnerable	Near Threatened	Least Concern

They often settle in **coral reefs** or meadows of sea grass.

Hungry Sea Horses

These **carnivores** have no teeth. Long **snouts** let sea horses suck up **prey**. Favorite foods include brine shrimp and other tiny **crustaceans**.

Sea horses do not have stomachs to **digest** food. They must eat all the time.

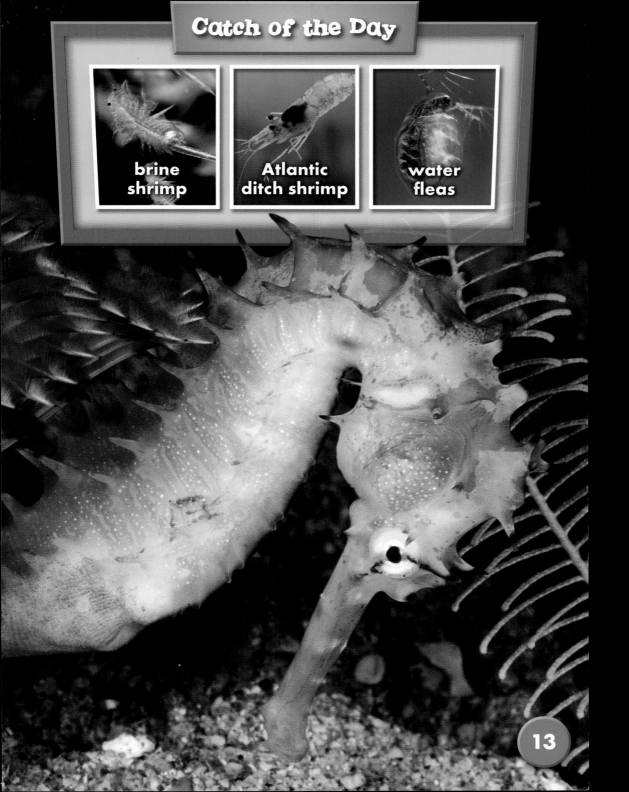

Catch of the Day

brine shrimp

Atlantic ditch shrimp

water fleas

Sea horses are slow swimmers. They usually try to stay in one place. Their tails hang on to **coral** or sea grass.

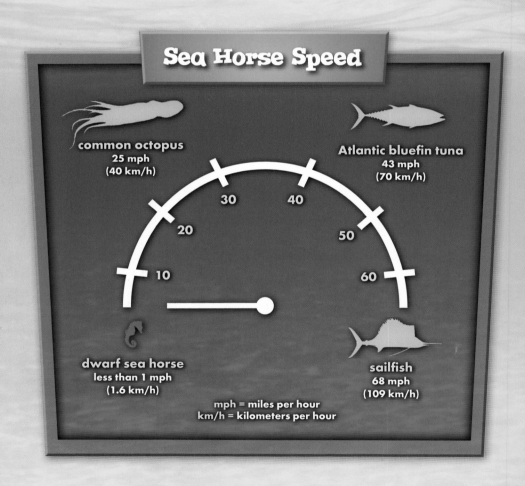

Sea Horse Speed

common octopus
25 mph
(40 km/h)

Atlantic bluefin tuna
43 mph
(70 km/h)

30 40
20 50
10 60

dwarf sea horse
less than 1 mph
(1.6 km/h)

sailfish
68 mph
(109 km/h)

mph = miles per hour
km/h = kilometers per hour

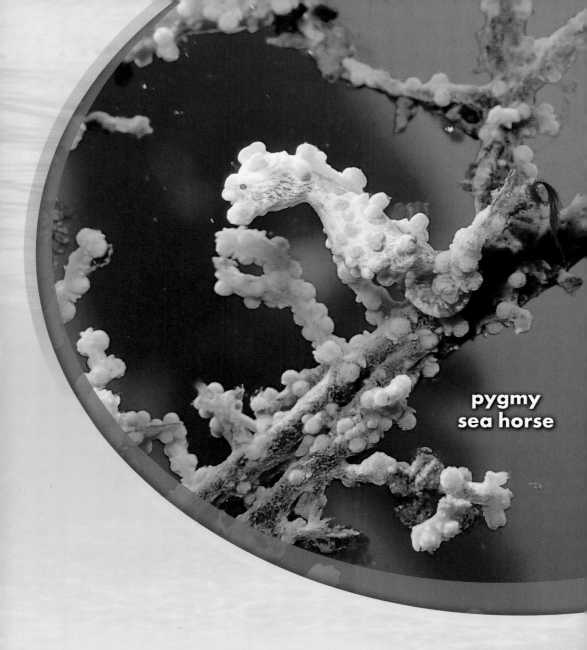

pygmy
sea horse

To hide, sea horses have **camouflage**. Some can even change colors!

Mates and Fry

Many sea horses stay with the same mate for life. They find each other through fancy **courtship displays**.

lined
sea horses

Males and females often change colors and dance to show interest. Then the two twist their tails together.

short-headed
sea horse

Courtship displays can last for hours or even days! At the end, the female puts her eggs in the male's pouch.

After a few weeks, the male gives birth to hundreds of babies.

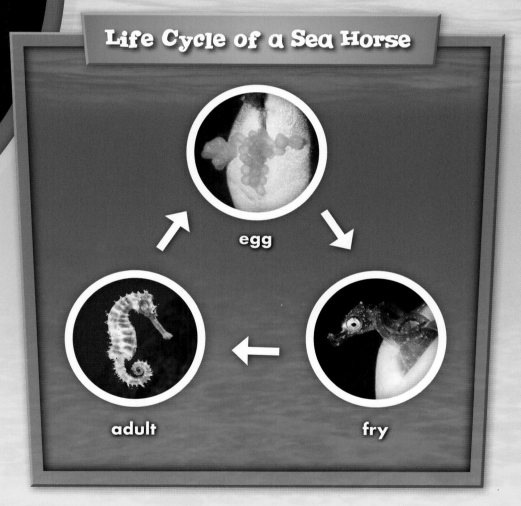

Life Cycle of a Sea Horse

egg

fry

adult

Baby sea horses, called **fry**, look like tiny adults. Most fry hold on to grass and coral to stay in place.

Some catch a ride on floating plants to find a new home!

Glossary

camouflage—a way of using color to blend in with surroundings

carnivores—animals that only eat meat

coral—the living ocean animals that build coral reefs

coral reefs—structures made of coral that usually grow in shallow seawater

courtship displays—behaviors that animals perform when choosing mates

crustaceans—animals that have several pairs of legs and hard outer shells; crabs and shrimp are types of crustaceans.

digest—to break down food so it can be used for the body

flexible—able to bend

fry—baby sea horses

grip—a tight hold

prey—animals that are hunted by other animals for food

snouts—the long noses and mouths of some animals

tropics—a hot region near the equator

To Learn More

AT THE LIBRARY

Curtis, Jennifer Keats. *Seahorses*. New York, N.Y.: Henry Holt, 2012.

MacQuitty, Dr. Miranda. *Eyewitness Ocean*. New York, N.Y.: DK Publishing, 2014.

Owen, Ruth. *Seahorse Fry*. New York, N.Y.: Bearport Pub., 2013.

ON THE WEB

Learning more about sea horses is as easy as 1, 2, 3.

1. Go to www.factsurfer.com.

2. Enter "sea horses" into the search box.

3. Click the "Surf" button and you will see a list of related web sites.

With factsurfer.com, finding more information is just a click away.

Index

The images in this book are reproduced through the courtesy of: Rich Carey, front cover; Nantawat Chotsuwan, p. 3; fenkieandreas, p. 4; Dirscherl Reinhard/ Glow Images, p. 5; Frolova_Elena, pp. 6, 7 (top left, top right, bottom), 19 (bottom left); Galina Savina, p. 7 (top center); Nature Picture Library/ SuperStock, pp. 9 (top), 10, 16; John Sear/ Wikipedia, p. 9 (bottom); Eric Isselee, p. 11; Napat, p. 13 (top left); Viridiflavus/ Wikipedia, p. 13 (top center); Lebendkulturen.de, p. 13 (top right); Minden Pictures/ SuperStock, p. 13 (bottom); Anne Frijling, p. 15; skynesher, p. 17; Oceanwide Images, pp. 18, 19 (top, bottom right); NHPA/ SuperStock, p. 20; Jane White/ Alamy, p. 21.